A Rainy Day

by Robin Nelson

BEGINNING
READER

It is a rainy day!

The rain is wet.

When it is rainy,
the sky is gray.

A rainy day is **gloomy.**

When it is rainy,
clouds fill the sky.

Raindrops fall from the clouds.

When it is rainy,
flowers grow.

We see a **rainbow.**

When it is rainy,
it can **flood.**

Lightning can strike.

When it is rainy,
rabbits hide.

Ducks swim in the rain.

When it is rainy,
we put on a raincoat.

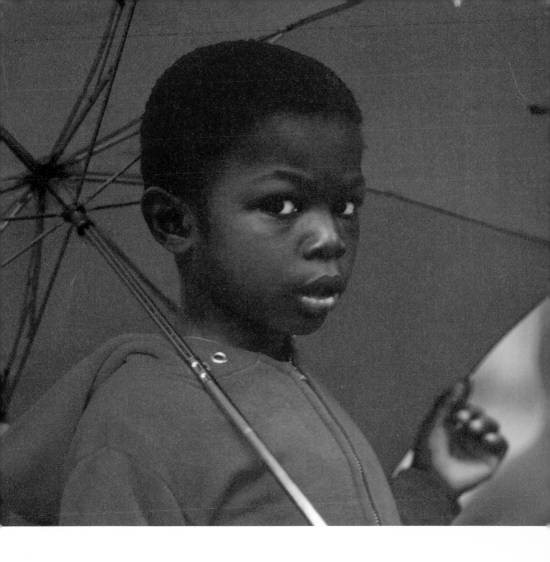

We open an umbrella.

When it is rainy,
we can splash.

A rainy day is fun!

The Water Cycle

The sun warms the water in the oceans. Heat changes the water from a liquid into a gas called water vapor. Water vapor rises into the sky. As the water vapor rises, it cools and forms tiny droplets. These droplets form a cloud. Inside a cloud, the water droplets combine. When the droplets combine, they get heavier and fall to Earth as rain. Rain runs into rivers, lakes, and oceans. Then the water cycle starts again.

Rainy Day Facts

One of the wettest places on Earth is Mount Wai'ale'ale in Hawaii. An average of 460 inches of rain falls there each year.

Louisiana is the wettest state in the United States. It gets about 56 inches of rain a year.

Freezing rain is rain that freezes when it hits the ground. Sleet is frozen ice pellets.

The heaviest raindrops fall as fast as 18 miles an hour.

Pinecones close up when it is going to rain.

Lightning makes the air so hot that it explodes. The sound it makes is called thunder.

Count the seconds between a flash of lightning and the sound of thunder. If there is a lot of time between the lightning and thunder, the storm is far away. If the lightning and thunder happen almost at the same time, the storm is very close.

Glossary

 clouds – masses of water droplets floating in the air

 flood – to overflow with water where it is usually dry

 gloomy – dull and dark

 lightning – a flash of electricity in the sky

 rainbow – an arch of colors that appears in the sky

Index

The photographs in this book are reproduced through the courtesy of: © Betty Crowell, front cover, pp. 6, 7, 22 (top); © Buddy Mays/TRAVELSTOCK, p. 2; © Walt Anderson/ © Visuals Unlimited, p. 3; © Michele Burgess, pp. 4, 9, 10, 22 (2nd from top and bottom); © Dee Read/Visuals Unlimited, pp. 5, 22 (center); © David Cavagnaro/Visuals Unlimited, p. 8; © Stephen Graham Photography, pp. 11, 22 (2nd from bottom); © Robert Fried, p. 12; © Robert C. Simpson/Visuals Unlimited, p. 13; © L.S. Stepanowicz/Visuals Unlimited, p. 14; © Annie Griffiths Belt/CORBIS, p. 15; © Ralph A. Clevenger/CORBIS, p. 16; © Joe Gemignani/CORBIS, p.17.

This book is available in two editions:
Library binding by Lerner Publications Company, a division of Lerner Publishing Group
Soft cover by First Avenue Editions, an imprint of Lerner Publishing Group
241 First Avenue North
Minneapolis, MN 55401 U.S.A.

Website address: www.lernerbooks.com

LIBRARY OF CONGRESS CATALOGING-IN-PUBLICATION DATA

Nelson, Robin.
    A rainy day / by Robin Nelson.
        p.   cm. — (First step nonfiction)
    Includes index.
    ISBN 0-8225-0173-2 (lib. bdg. : alk. paper)
    ISBN 0-8225-1962-3 (pbk. : alk. paper)
    1. Rain and rainfall—Juvenile literature. [1. Rain and rainfall.] I. Title.
II. Series.
QC924.7.N45 2002
551.57'7—dc21   00-012944

Manufactured in the United States of America
1 2 3 4 5 6 – AM – 07 06 05 04 03 02